DARE *to be* YOU

You were born to be **brave, bold** and **fabulous**

CATHY ALESSANDRA

Alessandra Group LLC
www.CathyAlessandra.com

Printed in the United States of America

Design: Carla Green, Clarity Designworks

ISBN 9781691916375

This book is dedicated to...

- The women around the world who are daring to live their YES... and the many more who want to.

- My wonderful new friends of Millport Scotland...thank you for welcoming me into your community.

- My family, friends and supporters who have been there through it all...I couldn't have done it without you.

Contents

Introduction

I'm writing this book from a two-bedroom flat in Millport Scotland. It's a small island, about 45 minutes by train outside of Glasgow, then a short walk to the ferry, a ten-minute ferry ride and another ten minutes further by bus. The town is about five blocks long and has approximately 1200 full time residents, but it is a beautiful magical place. I'd been twice before, once for a quick day trip in 2018, and again for Easter week in 2019. I was visiting a friend who lives here, and her beautiful second-level guest bedroom has a view of the town and harbor. One morning, as I sat pondering in prayer, I heard the call to come back. My intuition told me I needed to return for an extended period of time. And as luck would have it, an American woman at Easter dinner just happened to have the two-bedroom flat for sale or rent.

Now let me explain just a wee bit further... the two-bedroom flat sits on the top level of a wonderful old building that is on the waterfront. The main town street is all that is between me and the seafront benches. It has three windows in the living area, all facing the water. It was fully furnished and empty of tenants. The back of the building faces an old church. Actually, the old abandoned church towers over the building, in a protective way. The moment I walked in to check it out, I knew I needed to stay.

Explaining my "call" and decision to live in Scotland for the summer to family and friends was difficult. My kids, my parents, my boyfriend, my girlfriends... some had a very difficult time understanding and supporting my decision with a happy heart. My dad though, I think he got it. You see, my family heritage began here in Scotland. In fact, my grandfather was born here and the great-grandmother I'm named after is buried 16 miles as the seagull flies. But more than that, this trip was a calling to push the pause button and learn to just BE. Because you see, only in quieting my heart and mind, and BE-ing, was I able to hear.

This book was in my mind when I arrived, with a very different title and a slightly different focus. But being in magical Millport, the book settled into my heart. I found myself pondering, reflecting and wondering "what if", "should I" and "why". Like you, my life has had many twists and turns that make me wonder if the roller coaster is a joy ride or runaway train? But I've lived the last few years by the mantra and it has served me well. What is the mantra you ask?

YES I CAN.

I adopted that mantra back in 2013 when my life began to unravel at an alarming speed. It showed up in a gym on the Saturday before Thanksgiving on a t-shirt in bling sparkly writing. It said "One Woman Can." I'd just committed to trying to lose weight and get healthy for the millionth time – yes seriously the millionth. I looked at the shirt and said "HELL YEAH one woman can! I can! YES I CAN!" and my mantra was born.

Since that day, so much has changed. I've sold my two magazines, divorced after 29 years of marriage, launched a new business, sold a house of 20 + years, lost 70 + pounds, re-lost 25 pounds again, started over financially... and the list goes on. But I have not just survived. I have thrived.

How? By doing one simple thing. Living my YES... or living my TRUTH.

What does it mean to "live your YES"? It means taking everything from your bucket list to today's to-do list – and all your lists in between – to create a life you love living while building a business you love, or working in a career you love, or being a stay-at-home mom that you love. It's growing to become your best self, and in doing that, become the best wife or mother or girlfriend or sister or business owner.

It's time to stop living for everyone else's expectations of you. No more asking permission and comparing yourself. Put your oxygen mask on FIRST and stop waiting. You were born to be brave, bold and fabulous! Own the real you - YOUR dreams, your goals, your vision for your life – embody it, embrace it, live it and love it!

By now you may be thinking, "Wow Cathy, that sounds incredibly selfish. I've got kids, a husband, a job... I can't make big decisions like that on my own." Girlfriend listen up.... there is nothing selfish about truly living your YES. In fact, if you aren't living it, you are being selfish. Why? Because living in YES mode means living your truth and anything else would be a lie. It means living your truth in your relationships, your finances, and your business or career which allows you to be your best self. By being your best self, you give the love, time and attention to the things that matter most, in alignment with your core values. What could be better?

YES living is not unhealthy selfishness or self-centered decisions and it's certainly not self-indulgence. There is enough of that in our society's need of instant gratification and me, me me. It's living for the greater good of all - you, your family, your God given life purpose. It's learning to be content with less and to live in the present moment or experience. It's finding the joy in the mundane. And it's aligning it all with your core values. Ask yourself... Is this what I truly need or want? Does the direction feel right? Is it God's calling for me? How does it serve me and the greater good?

There is a lot of talk about balance being bull shit. And I'd have to agree. In my humble opinion, perfect balance as defined by our society is not a possibility. But there is intersection and integration, balance by your own definition and design. Living your YES is where home-life and work-life and all the other facets of YOUR life intersect, connect and integrate. The sooner you dare to master that, the sooner it will come to fruition.

Now don't get this confused with saying yes to everyone and everything. In fact, it's far from it. Daring to be you means strategic YESes and abundant NO's. It includes pillars, principles and steps that I strive to live by daily.

There are three words that became top in my vocabulary. Grace, grit and gratitude. What do those words have to do with it? Everything.

I went to hell and back – or at least it felt like it as I worked through my circumstances, my demons, my doubts and my setbacks. Grace, grit, gratitude – and God, transformed my life.

Grace – there are many definitions, but for my purposes, grace or blessings are given by God despite the fact I don't deserve them. Grace can be defined as extending kindness to the unworthy. My belief in God, a loving God, allows for grace and mercy which allows me to grow from my mistakes.

Grit – defined by strength and firmness of character; indomitable spirit; courage and resolve. Grit is when the going gets tough, the tough get going. It's the epitome of living with the mantra YES I CAN.

Gratitude – being in a place of gratitude for every success but also every setback, challenge and failure. I truly believe there is a lesson to be learned in all of it. Some lessons I'd rather have not experienced in the way that I did. Some days my gratitude is only that the sun is shining but striving to live in a place of unconditional gratitude allows me to get out of my own way and grow.

God – or Source. I believe in a higher power and for me that is God. He has shown his grace and mercy to me more than once. He has given me signs and messages in the form of friends and circumstances. I've seen it written in the sky and written on a chain link fence – that story to come. I've had dreams and downloads and when I am quiet, I can hear that still small voice. It means life is not always sunshine and roses, but no matter what, I am not alone.

PLEASE NOTE: Don't let the word God stop you from reading. If you believe in a power greater than yourself, whatever you call him or her, replace the word God with your belief. Universe, Buddha, The Divine, Goddess, Source. I see God as an all loving forgiving power greater than myself. But I know not everyone has had the same experience. Take it or leave it, but don't let it be an excuse to stop you from reading.

Throughout this book, I'll share stories and steps in how I was able to transform and rebuild my life at 50. These same steps can be the tools for you as well. I'll also share some of the lessons – from business, life, and God. The second part of this book is 30 Days of YES, a journey for you to "do the work" and find your transformation. I highly encourage you to participate in answering the questions posed along the way. Get a special journal or notebook, download the free resources mentioned along the way and commit to taking this journey. Maybe it's best for you to read it through once and come back to ponder the questions or maybe you read each chapter and answer the questions as you move along. But only in committing to do the work will you find your answers and ahas.

Take what you want, feel free to leave what doesn't work for you. But I promise if you do the work, the work will reveal your YES. Most importantly, get present – to the lessons, the learnings and your life.... Your YES life!

So, let's begin....

CHAPTER 1

....

Where does it begin?
The real story.

I'm no different than you. I put my big girl panties on one leg at a time. Some days it's lace and some days it's the iron clad, hold me together type. I have big dreams and bold goals. I get in a place of fear and worry and must pull myself out. But I get up every morning with a mantra... a mantra that moves me forward when I'm feeling stuck, a mantra that saves me from myself and my thoughts, a mantra that has made the difference between success and failure – my mantra is YES I CAN.

A little about me... I'm a California girl who grew up in Los Angeles. By all accounts, I had a charmed childhood. I was the typical high schooler who got into a little bit of trouble, like getting caught by my parents after drinking vodka at the high school dance. But all in all, I was a good kid with great parents.

Once I graduated from high school, I went off to college – for a year. After first semester with a 1.5 GPA, I brought the second semester GPA up to a 2.something... and at that point it was agreed I wouldn't return. One of my pivotal moments during that time period was when I was asked by a later-to-be in-law... "how I expected to hold an intelligent conversation with no college degree." That ladies and gentlemen, would be one of the first major limiting beliefs I would need to overcome. More on that later.

After marrying my high school sweetheart at 22, moving 5 times in eight years (one of those moves being overseas), and having my three kids by 31, I was a crazy busy mother and wife, PTA President, Girl Scout leader, fundraiser chair, room mom.... and business owner. I became "no" challenged. I said yes to everything – because I wanted to be liked, to be accepted, to be seen as a success – and I ultimately burned myself out.

I self-medicated with food. I was unhappy and stressed out and not finding the purpose of my life. I packed on the pounds as I stuffed my feelings of not being good enough, smart enough, pretty enough – you name it, I wasn't enough in anything.

But all that came to a screeching halt in 2013 when I began to discover my YES. Through a variety of circumstances, I was stopped in my tracks. I had to take a long hard look at me – and boy was that sobering. I had a child that was struggling, a marriage that was failing, a business that I was pouring my heart into not to mention being 216 pounds on a 5'2" frame with three different blood pressure pills I was taking daily. Can you say WAKE UP SISTER!!

I was encouraged to take an overnight solo retreat – yes, solo, by myself – with no phone, no computer, no TV – just to "be". That was the first of many solo retreats to come, but certainly the scariest. I wasn't comfortable being alone, but I had to do something. So there I was, in Santa Barbara CA – alone, with nothing to do except read the life-changing, now in retrospect *lifesaving* book, *The Four Agreements* by don Miguel Ruiz.

What are the four agreements, you ask? They are...

1. **Be impeccable with your word:** Speak with integrity. Say only what you mean. Avoid using the Word to speak against yourself or to gossip about others. Use the power of your Word in the direction of truth and love.

2. **Do not take things personally:** Nothing others do is because of you. What others say and do is a projection of their own reality, their own dream. When you are immune to the opinions and actions of others, you won't be the victim of needless suffering.

3. **Never make assumptions:** Find the courage to ask questions and to express what you really want. Communicate with others as clearly as you can to avoid misunderstandings, sadness and drama. With just this one agreement, you can completely transform your life.

4. **Always do your best:** Your best is going to change from moment to moment; it will be different when you are healthy as opposed to sick. Under any circumstance, simple do your best and you will avoid self-judgement, self-abuse and regret.

WOW!!! Those are powerful, aren't they? Even just writing them again reminds me how impactful living them can be. But here was the thing... in that moment, I realized I wasn't living by any of those agreements – and how shifting my thoughts and behaviors – MY thoughts and behaviors – could change my world. Here is how I related to each of the four agreements

Be impeccable with your word – I interpreted that to mean not only the gossip and talking about others, but also that little voice inside my head that would constantly say "who do you think you are? You can't do that. You're not good enough. You're not thin enough. You're not smart enough." It had to stop.

Do not take things personally – I was taking a lot of things personally. I think as women, we tend to do that more then men. We're defined by our children and their actions – or at least I was. When we aren't invited to something, we get our feelings hurt. And the list goes on. I learned that what other people think of me doesn't matter – that is their opinion. If I am living within my values, I am living my truth. Living by that agreement alone made a tremendous difference in my life.

Never make assumptions – It was time for me to ask the tough questions and clearly express my feelings. At the time, I was making a lot of assumptions in various areas of my life. Someone even said to me "I can't make you feel anything, but I sure can have fun trying." By being vulnerable and asking the tough questions, not making any assumptions, even if I didn't like the answer, that would shift my relationships.

Always do your best – my interpretation of this agreement was that those first three agreements were hard to live by 24/7. If I can do my best to live my life within those first three agreements, then maybe it would help me change the circumstances I was in – and they did.

Funny enough, while reading the book in Santa Barbara, I had the first of many God winks. I felt compelled to go to church – so I headed into downtown Santa Barbara and found Our Lady of Sorrows Catholic church. It was divine intervention as the message that night was focused on the same principles. He didn't quote the book, but the ideas were exactly the same.

What I learned that day was by changing my thoughts and behaviors, I could potentially change MY life, no one else's. I had been working to "fix" my child, "fix" my marriage, "fix" my body, "fix" my friends.... but I needed to fix me. As they say, I needed to put on my oxygen mask first before I could do anything for anyone else.

And THAT is where YES I CAN truly begins. That moment in time where I had the aha moment. It all began with me and my YES. And your life transformation begins with yours!

CHAPTER 2
....
What is YES I CAN all about?

YES I CAN consists of three pillars, four principles and five core areas.

The five core areas are: career and business, health and wellness, love and relationships, spirituality and service/leadership.

The four principles are: Be big, be bold, be brave, be bright.

The three pillars are: self-care, sacred space and support.

These make up everything yes. Let's dig into a bit of my story, what I discovered and how you can use these tools too.

The Five Core Areas

These are the five core areas that make up the YES foundation. On the YES wheel, you'll find these and others. Take a moment to look at each of these core areas and review, reflect and rate where you are in each area right now. This will give you your starting place.

To download your own free copy of the YES Wheel, go to: www.daretobeyoubook.com

Career/Business

Are you happy in your career? Are you working with passion and purpose? You may be an entrepreneur, a corporate businesswoman or a stay-at-home mom, but whoever you are, without these core areas in sync, you may always feel a wobble in your wheel.

Personal struggles are very much tied to our business success or lack thereof – and business struggles can be tied back to the personal issues. When I began my journey in 2008, I was unhappy in my personal life and had jumped into my business with both feet, working long hours, buried deep in my work, escaping my reality.

I began my first business in November of 1995, as an accidental entrepreneur with a three-year-old and an eight-month-old. I stumbled across a need in my community that wasn't being met, and I began my first magazine, What's Up For Kids with the idea of connecting parents with resources and things to do in our smaller community and immediately surrounding communities. What began as a four-page newsletter, copied on color paper with a circulation of 1000 was sold in 2015 as a 32-page full color glossy magazine with a circulation of 20,000.

Did I love my work? Absolutely! Was it a juggle? You bet. While I worked from home, being mom to three young kids plus cook, maid, taxi driver, volunteer and wife, I was publisher, editor, designer and delivery person – until I realized I needed help. When I began What's Up For Kids, I was filling a need that I new existed in my community. But I was also filling a personal need – the entrepreneurial desire and passion.

Over the years, that passion ebbed and flowed, and, in the summer of 2008, I was looking for what was next. My kids were in fact moving into high school with college around the corner. I'd been room mom, PTA President and all the other "titles" a mom could volunteer for… but something was shifting in me and I knew I was ready for the next step.

Through a variety of opportunities, I unknowingly opened my heart and mind to a journey of self-discovery that continues today. While continuing to publish the magazine, I tried several additional business ideas over the next few years – some of which were successful, others not so much. But the road is NEVER straight, is it?! There are always twists and turns, but the journey is the critical piece of the process. I had huge successes and catastrophic "failures". But I wouldn't be where I am today without taking those lessons with me. The failures and setbacks are part of the success. With each challenge and failure, I had learned something new. A door would close and a new one would open.

After selling my magazines, I stepped into the coaching world. I had coached or mentored many entrepreneurs in business and marketing for

YES
LIFE WHEEL

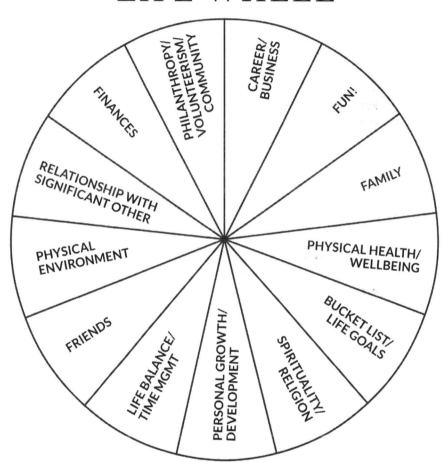

Rate your level of satisfaction for each area on a scale of 1-10, where 10 is the greatest satisfaction. Fill in the slice from the center outward, based on your rating. Sample for a rating of 5, fill the slice in from the center halfway to the outer edge..

CATHY ALESSANDRA
YES I CAN

free during those years of the magazine. I decided to take my business acumen and marketing expertise along with my life lessons and support other women in creating their YES I CAN life. Actually, it wasn't just a decision as such... but a discernment. I knew I needed to serve others by walking my talk and supporting them in their steps to wholeness, happiness and success.

Health and Wellness

You may be battling an illness or struggling to lose weight, but where does your happiness level rate when it comes to your health and wellness. Health and wellness are mind and body – so your physical health as well as your mental health. Are you discovering more about yourself by participating in self-development? Are you taking the steps necessary to take care of your physical body – eating healthy foods and moving daily?

My very first YES I CAN goal was health and wellness related. I was overweight, uncomfortable and taking medication to control weight-related high blood pressure. I made the decision – yes, committed to a decision to get healthy and feel better.

If you don't have your health, it's hard to live to your fullest potential. I understand sometimes we can't control our health-related circumstances, like a chronic disease or life-threatening illness, but there are things within our control to make the circumstance better and more tolerable. I'm not going to tell you to go out and exercise or lose weight or stop eating the junk food. What I am going to share is that when I did those things, my life began to shift. When I made the commitment to take care of me and my body, the vessel in which I get to spend my time here on earth, taking care of it like anything else that I expected to run for a lifetime, life changed.

When I started my health journey, I couldn't even walk for 30 minutes on a treadmill. But in 2018, I walked 75 + miles over six days on a pilgrimage in Spain – the Camino De Santiago. It started with small goals and a daily commitment to myself, to show up and work on being the best version of me I could be.

Health comes in many forms. Physical, emotional, mental... but it wasn't until I was willing to do the "work", daring to say YES I CAN, that I was able to begin the process of changing my life. The "work" was going to the gym, making healthy food choices... but the "work" was also the self-discovery and understanding of who I really was, inside and out, and how my past experiences were shaping my present reality.

Relationships

We have many relationships as we move through life, from our immediate family members and closest friends to our business associates and acquaintances. And don't forget your 5000 Facebook friends! For the purposes of YES I CAN, I've broken "relationships" into three categories.

The Sacred Circle

For me, this includes my three children and my parents. This is the group of the most important people in my life. I make the choice to give them my undivided time and attention when we are together – and I make the plans to be together! But it wasn't always that way.

As the world spins at an ever-increasing speed and we seem to be on our hand-held devices more and more, it's a choice to get present with the people right in front of us. When my children call and I'm working, I either stop what I'm doing, or I ask to call them back shortly – so I can give them my full undivided attention. When I'm with my boyfriend, I put my phone on silent and leave it in my purse. When I'm with someone I love and care about, I do my best to have uninterrupted quality time, putting my distractions aside!

While it may be easy to rationalize that they will understand if you can't take a moment with them because of say, a work deadline, the fact is they are the last people we should be putting off. These are the people who sometimes get moved to the bottom of the list to make time for those who really don't matter, because you think "they should understand". But you end up being too tired and stressed out because you are saying yes to everyone else. Can you say BACKWARDS!

While my "sacred" number is five, yours may be different. You may or may not have kids, a spouse or extended family. But I challenge you to determine who they are, the ones who are MOST important to you in the whole world. They are the ones who require and deserve your time, love, understanding and nurturing.

Within the "sacred" number, you may have a spouse or significant other: I was married almost 30 years before my divorce. And maybe if I had learned some of these lessons early on, we'd still be married. Marriage is a two-way street and joint effort and if you are not willing to do the work, it's easy to pull apart.

A successful love relationship takes effort. When you are in the flow and the areas of your life are filled with joy and happiness, the bumps in the road and the twists and turns in life are easier to tackle, together. But when challenges arise and you are not aligned, it becomes almost impossible. Practice vulnerability with each other, learning to share openly about your business, your personal needs, your desires, your fears… all of that allows for a deeper, solid connection.

The Inner Circle

The inner circle is the next group of people in your life. It's typically a handful of close friends or family. These are the relationships with mutual respect and support. They are the people who hold you up, champion you, laugh with you, cry with you, support you, and love you unconditionally with no judgement. These are the people you would do anything for – and they would do anything for you.

Why do you need to know who is in your "sacred" and "inner" circles? Because when you are making decisions on where, when, how and with whom to spend your time, energy and commitment, you make sure to give these people priority! These relationships DO NOT suffer at the expense of other commitments.

Everyone else

The rest is gravy. They may be in your life for a specific reason, a season or a lesson. But their expectations and demands are not meant for you to hold on to.

Dr. Seuss said it best… "Be who you are and say what you feel, because those who mind don't matter and those who matter don't mind." I am reminded of this repeatedly as I am challenged by those who really don't matter.

Over the years, I've struggled with this group of relationships. The more successful and excited you are about who you are becoming and what you are doing or creating, the bigger the line in the sand becomes as to who is a real friend and supports and champions you. There are those who want you to stay the same, play small, fear your change and won't truly support your potential as you dare to grow.

As you change and transform to your full potential, being bold in your thoughts, ideas and actions, having big dreams for your life, daring to be the real you in the process, there will be those who just can't support you and will try to tear you down. Being the real you means putting your ideas and beliefs out there – not ideas just to appease others. Not everyone will agree with your opinions, your actions or your behavior. But in my humble opinion, this typically comes from their insecurities and shortcomings. It's easier for them to "hate", complain and "bitch" then to look at themselves in the mirror. Their reality may just be too painful.

Your relationship with you....

Whether you are single, married, divorced, widowed, dating or done, the relationship part of YES I CAN begins with loving yourself, unconditionally, so you can love others. To be in relationship, the sacred or inner circle kind, requires presence and emotional support in both directions.

Do you love yourself? Unconditionally? We berate ourselves, judge ourselves, stop ourselves – out of fear, doubt, discomfort and sometimes disdain. Loving ourselves is the hardest part. Our body, our mind, our ideas... self-love is harder than "loving" anyone else. But if we practice self-love – being kind, gracious, compassionate and forgiving of ourselves - we can experience self-love, which in turn allows us to truly give love. Dare to love yourself unconditionally.

Spirituality

Spirituality takes many forms and for you it may take no form at all. I believe in a power greater than myself. For me, that power is God. But for you it may be Buddha, the Dali Lama, Spirit, Source, or The Universe.

Do you spend time in prayer, meditation, journaling or expanding your faith, whatever faith is to you?

In my darkest days, I was grateful to rediscover my relationship with God. I'd grown up in a church household. My grandfather was a Presbyterian minister and we went to church every Sunday. Religion was modeled but it wasn't until my life was unraveling that I discovered my faith. Faith is believing in something you can't see or touch – believing there is a greater good, a greater outcome, a lesson to be learned from everything. Faith is the belief that God has my back and while I might not like the outcome of a situation, it's for the greater good.

Routines and Rituals: I begin every day reading scripture and a devotional, I may pull an angel card or three, I journal as a thought process and discussion with God – and then… wait for it… I listen. I do my best to be aware of signs around me, experiences and circumstances, and I watch and participate as God shows up in my life. During a particularly difficult time, I was woken by His voice.

I was on a cruise ship, in a cabin by myself but traveling with my parents. We were arriving the next morning in Norway and I was reminded to set my alarm and not be late. But I was awoken to someone banging on my door, calling out to me… "Cathy, Cathy, wake up." In my groggy sleepy state, I flew out of bed, ran to the door and opened it expecting my father… but there was NO ONE there! Not a soul anywhere to be seen up and down the halls. I closed the door and turned around to glance at the clock. It was before 5am, but the sun was up and streaming through my slightly open curtains. Upon pulling the curtains open and walking onto the balcony, I saw the majestic mountains, the waterfalls, our huge multi-ton cruise ship gliding through the fjord in total peace. It was God, waking me out of my sorrowful, self-pity state saying "Don't miss this Cathy, don't miss your life. The abundance is all around you. Be at peace and see the beauty in everything." I can't even begin to explain the feeling of calm and connection. For some of you, you'll be thinking "she's crazy". But there are plenty more God moments like it! It's how I roll and what I believe, and we don't have to agree. Being fully open to the Spirit gives me peace and hope in all of life's challenges and celebrations. I'm not in charge – He is.

Leadership/Service

Whether a leader in your community, around the world or in your own home, you cannot be a leader of others until you truly learn to lead from within. That begins by living your life in alignment with your core values.

What are your core values? Mine are faith, family, freedom and making a difference – in that order. (You can download the YES values exercise at: www.daretobeyoubook.com) My decisions and actions are based on those values. I walk my talk and lead by example. I learned early on in my journey that until I started living my life in alignment with my core values, leading by example, I would never attract the right people into my life. That goes for business contacts and personal relationships, clients and friends.

There are many leadership roles in your life...as a parent, a friend, a mentor, as the leader of your "tribe" as well as volunteer service. Once you can lead from within, it's time to lead others. That means paying it forward and giving back, serving others in a way that only you can serve and bringing out the gifts in others. I wholeheartedly believe in service – volunteer service. Giving of one's time, talents and treasure not only helps others but can bring you great joy.

Many of us are "in service" to others in our chosen career. But I'm talking about being "of service" with no monetary compensation. We have all been given gifts – an experience, specialty or calling. Using that to give back and pay it forward to others is, in my humble opinion, a requirement of the gift of this life. It may be as simple as a smile to a homeless person sitting on the corner or as complex as leading a philanthropic organization but being of service can be one of life's greatest rewards and bring riches beyond measure.

Using your pain for possibility is one of the many ways to serve others. I divorced after 29 years of marriage. I'm grateful it was an amicable divorce, but it was painful, nonetheless. I had comfort from many but truthfully, only if you have been through a divorce do you understand the pain. I searched for support groups, knowing support is critical when going through anything. But I also knew I needed the right group who would understand my pain. After many months of searching and not finding one, it was suggested I begin a support group at my church. I am a trained life coach and Stephen's Minister. Could I facilitate it? Yes. Would I get the support I desired? Yes. I could take my pain and be of service.

How can you lead and be "of service"? Some donate thousands to a charity that speaks to their heart. And while I believe in giving my treasure and do, I more often give my time and talents. Consider volunteering in an area or a cause that speaks to your heart – for me that was starting a divorce support group, cooking meals for homeless youth in

Los Angeles and chairing a fundraiser for breast cancer programs at my local hospital. What speaks to you? How can you dare to lead and serve?

Life Goals

The last area is your life goals. This includes things on your bucket list, your dream list and your "life" list. It includes everything else important to you in your pursuit of passion and purpose that hasn't already been covered.

For me it includes things like travel and owning a home. But it's imperative to speak it. It's your truth, your YES. If you have a dream, it may never come to fruition if it isn't spoken. My "life" list included walking the pilgrimage of the Camino de Santiago trail and traveling to Scotland with my father. It includes an African safari and taking my kids and their kids (kids not yet even a twinkle in their parent's eye) on vacations. It includes buying my forever home.

Have you heard of the Camino de Santiago trail? It winds from France to Spain and is the trail that St James walked on pilgrimage. When I heard about it, I was mesmerized. I read about it, watched a movie with Martin Sheen about it (*The Way* – I highly recommend it) and felt called to walk it as a must-do spiritual journey, so and it was added to my bucket list. I talked about it, sharing my dream with others. If you walk the whole trail, its 500km and takes about 30 days. But you can begin in Sarria, Spain and walk the last 100 km taking approximately six days. One of my best friends knew this was important to me and nudged me along to meet with a travel agent. Lo and behold, we met, made the plan and I had nine others join the trip. For me, it was a spiritual journey of forgiveness and letting go, one that I will never forget. For others, it was a trip of accomplishment, walking 18 miles the first day and completing the 75 + miles over the week.

What is on your life goals list? Writing a book, traveling the world, living in a foreign country …experiencing what? We are meant to have dreams and goals. I don't believe we would be given these dreams if they weren't possible. However, wishing and hoping will not bring the dream to fulfillment. But doing the work and speaking it will get you one step closer.

THE YES WHEEL

Now that you understand the five core areas, it's time to do a little work, rating each area for satisfaction. There are more than just these five areas on the wheel and there are no right or wrong answers. This is a starting point for you. When I complete the exercise, and I do it regularly, things change and I can adjust my focus and time based on my answers. You may be feeling discontent and unhappiness and not even realize where it's coming from or why. And until you peel back the layers like this, you won't.

Many years ago, I had buried myself in my work. I loved it. I'd work all day and all night and dream up and brainstorm new things all the time. I was busy, busy, busy. But what I really was, was unhappy and discontent in a variety of these areas. It was easier to bury myself in my work rather then review, reflect and reboot my life. When I took stock, peeling back the layers, it allowed me to see where I was truly struggling – and work on that. It allowed me to discover my purpose and dare to be me.

Download the YES Wheel for free at: www.DareToBeYoubook.com.

After reviewing your YES Life Wheel, the next step is understanding the principles.

The Four Principles

Principle #1 – Be BIG!

This is your BIG vision in all areas of your life. It's the vision of who you are, why you want to be that, how you are going to show up in life, and when you're going to start. When I looked at this first principle, I needed faith in my dreams and my goals. Thinking big requires you to get outside your comfort zone – getting comfortable being uncomfortable. I had to peel back the layers and discern my greater purpose and bigger calling. I had to dare to be me. It takes time to enter the process and go through the discovery. This wasn't and isn't an overnight process – but the outcome and understanding far outweighs the work that must be done.

What does this mean for you? It means dreaming. What do you want your life to look like in five years, ten years, next year? Are you starting or growing a business or taking the next leap in your career?

What are your financial goals? How will you accomplish them? Are you desiring a love relationship, or a better marriage? Maybe it's friends and the desire to have deeper connections. Spiritually speaking, what does it mean to be big? A closer connection with God or a better understanding of the Universal Laws?

> *Take ten minutes to "hot pen." What is "hot penning?" It is setting a timer and writing, never lifting your pen from the paper until the timer goes off. If you aren't sure what to write, write "I don't know what to write, I don't know what to write" as many times as necessary until the real words and feelings begin to pour out – and they will. The first time I experienced hot penning was the first time I really took a deep dive into my feelings. Grab a special notebook or journal, set the timer and go.*

HOT PEN QUESTIONS: What is the BIG vision for your life? What are your dreams? Dare to spell it out in detail, being specific about where are you living, who is in your life, what passions you are pursuing, and so on....

Principle #2 – Be BOLD

Once I understood my big vision, it was time to own it in a bold way. It required confidence and grit. It means bold decisions and actions when others may not agree with you. It means being who you are meant to be and not hiding or playing small. It means finding your voice and being totally authentically aligned with what you are doing, saying and being. It truly means daring to be the real you.

As I've moved into fully living my YES every day, being bold has required me to stretch in ways I never thought possible. Remember, I'm writing this book in Scotland. I felt *called* to return. Called, you ask? Yes, my Divine inner guidance system said I needed to return. Funny enough, when I was here at Easter in 2019, I fell and broke my knee cap. Was that a message I wasn't to come back? No, I heard it as a warning to slow down and just BE. The people in my life at the time were shocked, stunned and surprised. Scotland – why? And in all honesty, I couldn't explain. But I knew there was a reason that had not yet been revealed – even if it was just to "BE" for two months, which eventually was extended to three months. So off I went – in a very bold decision to head to another continent on my own. And not surprisingly, more revealed itself every day.

Don't worry about what other people think or their expectations of you. When you are willing to be bold, life is attracted to you. You don't need permission from others. You don't need acceptance from others. You need to dare to say YES to the calling in your heart and be bold in going after it.

Take ten minutes to "hot pen".

HOT PEN QUESTIONS: How are you being BOLD in your life? Are there dreams and goals in your heart, but your head tells you to stop. Are you playing small to adjust to the expectations of others? Why? What is one bold move you are ready to make now?

Principle #3 - Be BRAVE

Being brave is scary, isn't it?! It's facing the demons or the monsters under the bed at night. Truthfully, it's facing your greatest fears, head on. Courage, grit and tenacity are required. I found it easier if I was able to take that fear and convert it into my fuel for change.

There are many challenges we face daily. And many of our everyday fears are easily faced if being brave becomes a habit. When looking at living your YES, including your career, your relationships and your health, are you really doing the brave thing? Or are you hiding, doing only the minimum so that you can sidestep the fear?

A question that has been posed to me many times over the years is "what are you pretending not to know?" That is where bravery must begin – facing the fear that you've buried deep within the recesses of your soul.

Take ten minutes to "hot pen".

> **HOT PEN QUESTIONS:** How are you being BRAVE in the various areas of your life? How can you make fear your fuel? What's the greatest fear you have today, right now in this moment, that you can convert into fuel, so as to reach your goals and dreams?

Principle #4 - Be BRIGHT

Being bright is resilience, period. It's allowing your light to shine through even on the darkest of days. Whatever challenges and obstacles you are facing, it's having the resilience to turn it around and see the light at the end of the tunnel. Everyone, and I mean EVERYONE is facing something. It may be small, or it may be huge and overwhelming, but everyone is going through something. And it's in how we respond, not react, that we can allow our light to shine.

I understand we can get stuck in a pity party. I have. Where the "woe is me" comes through. And maybe a quick pity party is permissible. But when we get stuck in the pity party – day after day, week after week, month after month - talking about it, moaning about it and not doing anything about it – THAT will dull any light. Keep moving. Take one tiny step forward every day – forcing yourself to move, not allowing yourself to get stuck. Things will shift; your perspective, your circumstances, your life.

Take ten minutes to "hot pen".

> **HOT PEN QUESTIONS:** Are you being resilient? Or are you stuck in the muck of a full-blown pity party? What is the one step, even the tiniest little step, you can dare to take right now, today – and tomorrow and the next day, that can change everything?

The BONUS principle - Dare to BE YOU!

Stop comparing yourself. Stop trying to be something or someone you are not. You are exactly who you are meant to be. You are perfect just

as you are. We get in our head, we make decisions based on the expectations of others, and we try to be someone we were never meant to be.
The sooner you OWN who you truly are on the inside and are meant to
be on the outside, the faster you will find the joy in everything.

There is no one else created to do the things YOU were born to do.
Don't compare, don't compete, just BE YOU in everything you do. Fact
is, if you don't honor who you truly are, regret will inevitably follow. I
don't know about you, but I do not want to be at the end of my life with
a list of woulda's, coulda's and shoulda's. You were born to be brave,
bold and fabulous!

The Three Pillars

The three pillars are the game changers and foundation of everything
YES. November 2013 was truly the perfect storm for me. It had been
brewing for years. The dark clouds had gathered overhead, there was
thunder and lighting, and the wind was whipping all around me like a
hurricane. I was standing in an open field – no shelter, no place to run
and hide, not even an umbrella. But that pinnacle moment was exactly
where I needed to be to begin to make the incredible shifts in my life.

I have no doubt that Divine intervention is at work in my life. God
allowed me to stand in the storm just long enough to see that I couldn't
do it alone and that I must get to the heart of what really mattered.
It was a reminder of who is really in charge and that He is with me,
always. It has been shown to me over and over again, in signs, experiences, and "coincidences". And that's how the three pillars begin.

These three pillars are what YES I CAN is built on. They hold the
foundation for everything else. When one pillar falters, the others begin
to crack. Like a three-legged easel, they must all be in place to stand
firm.

Picture an easel. It has three "legs" that hold up whatever is on it.
What if the canvas sitting on the easel is your life picture? You have this
beautifully painted canvas sitting on an easel that is tilting over and
with one light breeze, it will fall. Or maybe you have a fabulous canvas
that is blank. Nothing on it. It's waiting for the bright, brilliant, bold
colors of your life transformation to be painted. But it needs the three
legs to hold it steady – or it will come crashing down.

The three pillars are: Self-Care, Sacred Space and Support.

Self-Care

Yes, self-care can mean a massage or mani/pedi. But I'm talking about it from a much deeper level. Self-care is everything you do to nourish your mind, body and soul. Do you have a morning ritual or routine? How about an evening one? Are you taking time alone – in silence and solitude, to ponder and pray.

Self-care is all about taking care of you and making you the #1 priority. It's about setting the intention and boldly acting on it – doing whatever it takes. It is not selfish as society can lead us to believe. It's essential as you cannot be your best self for others if you aren't taking care of you. You can't pour into others from an empty pot.

In each of the core areas, there is self-care.

Career/Business

What does self-care look like in business? First, it's not making your business your #1 priority. Yes, you read that right! YOU are the first priority – not your company or career. It's not live to work, but work to live.

Self-care in business includes working ON your business, not IN it. We get so busy with the day to day grind that we sometimes forget to pick our head up long enough to see where the road is leading. We may have gotten off course and need to course correct, but we aren't aware of that unless we give our business a little self-care. A few suggestions for business self-care include:

- Take a quarterly solo-retreat. I highly recommend getting out of your usual environment for this. I firmly believe the saying – "A change of pace + a change of place = a change of perspective." Get your profit and loss statement, bring your goals, bring big pads of paper and markers – and dream. This is an opportunity to review what is working, decide if there is something new to add or tweak and get ready for what's next.

- Attend events with other entrepreneurs and co-workers. There are 1000's of events around the country and many are in your niche. You can attend events for inspiration, to keep up with the latest tools and technology in your industry or just to connect with other like-minded entrepreneurs to brainstorm.

- Join a mastermind. Along the lines of being with like-minded entrepreneurs or business associates, a mastermind is a great way to connect in a safe environment and get the feedback you need on new ideas, products and growth. Think of it as a think tank or brain trust. Some of my greatest "aha-s" have come out of masterminding.

How can you commit to business self-care?

Health and Wellness

Self-care includes mental and physical health. This is everything from keeping up with your annual doctor visits to eating healthy foods and moving your body daily. And, of course, the occasional mani-pedi! Your physical health will impact your mental and emotional health – and vice versa. If you want your body to run at optimum speed, you need to give it first class care!

A few suggestions for health and wellness self-care include:

- At the beginning of each year, schedule all annual preventative check-ups. From mammograms to your teeth cleaning, it's important to keep your body in tip-top shape.

- Your body will run better with healthy fuel. Eating clean, healthy whole foods nurtures your body from the inside out. Movement is also necessary. Whether a daily walk or weekly gym visit, move your body.

- Ok, yes - a mani-pedi, massage or other treat is a great self-care remedy.

How will you commit to health and wellness self-care?

Relationships

Relationships require self-care. I realized early in my journey that I needed to work on me and my part of the relationship. I worked on it from my side with no expectations of the outcome. After all, I can't control someone else in a relationship – only myself and my expectations. But in changing the way I respond, it allows others to either accept me for who I am ... or not.

Suggestions for relationship self-care includes:

- Date night. If you are married or have a significant other, making time regularly to nurture the relationship is critical. However, this also goes for anyone in that sacred circle. I have special times with my children as well – each of them individually.

- Girlfriend time. Girlfriends can be a bond of sisterhood. Some of my deepest relationships and greatest times are with girlfriends. Having a GNO (girls' night out) or even a girls-getaway weekend can refresh and reboot not only the relationship, but you!

- "Group" care. Remember the list of all the "other" relationships? Just because they aren't in your sacred or inner circle doesn't mean you don't need to spend time or nurture those acquaintances. After all, building the "know, like and trust" factor is a great way to build your business and friendships. Bringing larger groups together or attending functions with these groups to stay connected is great self-care. There can be high energy, great brainstorming, lots of laughs and new connections made. And it's done in a group – saving you precious "individual" time for those that matter most. Connecting regularly with new friendships can lead to closer relationships.

What relationships in your life need the most self-care right now? Commit to something each month.

Spirituality

Self-care in spiritually can be found in several rituals and routines. For some, it may be attending church or a religious center. For others, it's spending time alone in silence and solitude. Over the last few years, I have created a few rituals and routines in my spiritual self-care that have allowed me to grow in my faith. Explore what "faith" and spirituality mean to you and if and how you want to live it.

Suggestions for self-care in your spiritual life include:

- Find a church or spiritual center and inquire about study, meditation or prayer groups.

- Commit to creating time and space for prayer, pondering and listening.

- Explore taking a spiritual retreat. Whether a pilgrimage in Spain or local retreat in the mountains, whether led by someone or on your own, explore the idea of getting out of the daily "grind" and into a place of BE-ing and listening.

Sacred Space

Sacred space includes your physical space and virtual space, as well as emotional and relational boundaries.

Physical space: Have you created a space to work? To create? To be alone? Your surroundings need to reflect you. I have created an office I love – surrounded by beautiful things, pictures, pillows and accessories. I've created a bedroom I love – in colors that align with what fills me with peace, nurturing and love. I have created a special place in my home for my prayer time – with a comfortable chair, my journal, special pictures and my Bible.

How can you create a sacred space for you?

Relational space: Have you ever felt overwhelmed and suffocated by being around others? Have you ever felt your positive energy quite literally be drained from you by the negativity of others? I have – and it doesn't feel good. This is when boundaries are essential.

There are those in your life who are energy vampires. They suck the positive right out of your idea, the room or your life. Their negative energy is swirling and their need to bring you into it can feel daunting. And yet most of the time, they are totally unaware of it. They could be friends, family members or your spouse/significant other. Knowing your boundaries and learning what this feeling is and how to detach in love can save you from the exhaustion of their vibe.

Who are your energy vampires? How can you lovingly put up a boundary?

Emotional space: Let's face it, the world can be a crazy, chaotic place. Life happens and sometimes we just need our space to deal with the emotions. (NOTE: There is a difference between healthy emotional space and cutting yourself off from everyone and not processing the feelings. If you struggle in this way, my heart reaches to you and I ask you to please seek professional help and support.) There is a need at times to step outside the chaos and go within.

I've found myself in the spot of needing to go within a few times in my life. When my son left for rehab, something he had asked for, I went deep within – for about three days. I couldn't talk on the phone, I wouldn't see anyone, I could text... sometimes. I laid on his bed and cried. On day three, a knock at the door revealed three girlfriends who had come by to literally pick me up off the floor and just be with me.

I also needed emotional space around the time of my divorce. I needed to go within and not share with everyone. I needed to honor my energy and not explain or discuss anything. I put the boundaries in place so that I could process what I needed to, when I needed to, with support IF I needed it.

When have you needed emotional boundaries? Is there something now you need a boundary around?

Virtual space: How are you keeping virtual boundaries? In this world of emails, social media, text and expectations of immediate gratification and response, it can be hard to find that sweet spot of space. I don't respond to email or social media when I first get up. Instead I spend time in my rituals and routines of writing, pondering and praying. We can get sucked into the frenzy of the day if we don't hold our virtual boundaries – comparing ourselves with others on social media, allowing someone's demands via email to take us in a direction we hadn't anticipated, or a reaction to a text message.

What can you do to hold your virtual space?

Support
Fact: we are NOT meant to do this thing called "life" alone. Support groups, mentors, coaches, therapists, friends... there is a reason they all exist and it's up to us to stop being the martyr and accept the support. Here are a few ideas for support:

Business/Career

- Find a mastermind group – search for one in your local community or start one. I found great support to brainstorm ideas and get constructive feedback on my business ideas by meeting with like-minded entrepreneurs. Can't find one? Start one!

- Hire a coach – do your research and find a qualified coach to support your growth. The International Coach Federation has a list of qualified, certified coaches. Many call themselves a coach but haven't really done the work. Do your homework – and hire the best possible fit.

Health/Wellness

- Research the health care practitioner that will support you and make an appointment.

- Need help with a workout? Hire a coach or trainer. Find one who will create a program for your specific goals and needs. A health coach can be a great addition if you are looking for support in nutrition and accountability to reach your goals.

- Join an online community. There are many options on top social media platforms for health and wellness support. Depending upon the group and reason for joining, review their privacy policies.

Relationships

- Therapist – whether you are in a relationship that is struggling or not, hiring a therapist to work though personal issues can be of great benefit. If your marriage or significant other relationship is struggling, invite your partner to join therapy with you.

- Support group – you may find yourself in a relationship where you personally need outside support. When my son was struggling, I attended AlAnon meetings. What a blessing. Find group support that supports you.

Spirituality

- Are you looking to expand your faith? There are many spiritual groups for bible study or exploring one's faith. Find the one that works for you.

- Are you questioning your faith? Maybe a conversation with a spiritual leader would help. This could be a minister, priest or spiritual counselor.

Self-care, sacred space and support. Can you see how these pillars provide you the foundation for everything you want to accomplish? They are truly critical to your overall success. You must make you a priority, learning to put boundaries into place, learning to say yes strategically and no abundantly, and creating the space you need to flourish. You must have people in your life who will support you, cheering you on when things get tough, challenging you when things get too easy, and loving you for exactly who you dare to be.

CHAPTER 3

The Lessons

Ahh, the lessons. There are so many, too many to even begin to share. But we'll start with the top lessons from my transformation and how you might be able to use them in your life.

Lesson 1: Strategic YESes and abundant NOs

Let's start with the most important lesson - strategic YESes and abundant NOs. I was NO challenged. I was a self-professed no challenged woman. I had FOMO (fear of missing out) so I said YES to everything. I wanted to be liked, seen as successful, and in the know. By saying yes to everything, I missed out on what was most important. I'll never forget the day…as my son's class left via bus for a field trip. I stood there in the school parking lot crying, so wanting to go with him, his class and the other parents. But I had said YES to so many other things that I had to say no to that special time with my son. I doubt he would remember, but I do.

I've had many say to me "but Cathy, you are the YES I CAN coach. How can you say no?" My answer – strategic YESes and abundant NOs. As you work through this book, you'll reaffirm your values and priorities. It's learning to stop and check in with yourself before saying yes to anything. When I'm asked to do something, I quickly ask myself if it is aligned with my values. Will it take time away from my family? Will it jeopardize my freedom? Will it be making a difference? Sometimes it requires further thought and ponder, and when it does, don't be afraid to say, "may I get back to you on that."

My life lesson appeared when I realized I had sold my soul to make others happy. As you work through this process and become more aware of your values and goals and your commitments versus obligations, your yes and no decisions will become much easier.

Dare to say no, abundantly. It is a complete sentence.

Lesson 2: Stop waiting for ready or perfect. Good is good enough.

Why are you waiting? What are you waiting for... the perfect job, the perfect mate, the perfect moment? Quit the procrastination. Make you a priority. Make your YES the first thing on your to-do list, not the "if I get around to it". As women, we tend to take care of everyone else – never putting on our own oxygen mask, and then nearly passing out from the lack of oxygen and energy.

I had waited – and waited and waited – for the right time, the right place, the right person. I had waited to be better, richer and thinner. But why? As I shared earlier, my biggest lesson was that I needed to stop waiting to take care of ME! I was trying to fix everyone and everything else, waiting for the right time for me, and it nearly killed me.

Along with stop waiting, believe that good is good enough. Life is short. You aren't promised next year, next week or tomorrow. You have this moment in time. Don't wait for perfect – it won't come. Don't wait for a better time, it may never arrive. Don't wait for next year because who knows what next year will bring. Dare to live the life you were meant to live. Waiting for perfect or ready will get you nowhere.

Dare to stop waiting.

Lesson 3: Own your worth and value.

This is a tough concept for many women and one I personally grappled with for years. Owning my worth and my value, and getting paid for it. As a woman entrepreneur with a huge heart, I wanted to help anyone and everyone. I wanted to see others succeed. I wanted to offer help wherever I could. I would give away my services and discount myself. But why? Did I not deserve to be compensated fairly?

To work through this and get comfortable charging what I was worth, I had to discover why I had this "story". Where had I learned I wasn't worthy? Where had I learned I wasn't good enough to charge for my service. In doing the inner digging, it went back to that moment I shared at the beginning of the book – the family member who asked me "how do you expect to hold an intelligent conversation without a college degree?"

Yes, it's true. I have no college degree. I went for a year and basically failed out. No worries – except that I held on to the comment for years and kept it a secret that I had no degree. When the subject would come up, I'd quickly change it or walk away. I didn't even tell my kids. Until I had the epiphany. WHY was I allowing a piece of paper to dictate who I was and whether I was successful or not?

Higher education and a college degree are held in high regard by me, my family and my community. I fully respect the education system and understand there are many careers where it is required. We encouraged our children to pursue a college education and in fact, two of them did, one graduating Magna Cum Laude and the other Suma Cum Laude. One chose the no college path.

While I understood the importance of a college education for some, I also realized that I could be successful without one, and I'd already proven that. I learned big lessons in the classroom of life. But I let that piece of paper define me. And in fact, I'm doing more with my life then some who hold a degree!

There are a few very recognizable names of highly successful entrepreneurs who share this status with me. Rachel Ray, famous chef and TV personality; Mary Kay Ash, Founder of Mary Kay Cosmetics; Debbie Fields of Mrs. Fields Cookies. And let's not forget the men... Wolfgang Puck, Walt Disney, Bill Gates of Microsoft and Michael Dell of Dell Computers. I'm fine graduating from the same higher education as they did – the School of Hard Knocks and Life Lessons!

Dare to own your worth and value – in all areas of your life. Charge what you are worth. Ask for the raise. Dig to discover the story and write a different ending.

Lesson 4: Failure is not failure unless you quit.

In every "failure", there is a lesson to be learned. I wholeheartedly believe that. I've had great success in life and some catastrophic "failures". But in taking a moment to review, reflect and reboot, I'm able to take the lesson on to the next endeavor or opportunity or experience.

One such "failure" was a business endeavor. I launched the National Association of Entrepreneur Moms. I beat my head against a wall for two years. I knew I had done everything, tried everything and it was draining my energy. I had all kinds of free members, but very few were paying for the services we were offering. Was it a flop? Was I a failure? How would I position that?

One day, my business coach asked me a simple question, "what if you turned it into a magazine?" DUH! I already had a very successful magazine. What if I had two – and the economies of scale with two?! (This is why having a coach is critical – if they are good, they can see the big things you are too focused to see.) While I did have that momentary thought of "failure", I quickly recognized that I wasn't serving the community in the way I was meant to serve. They weren't getting and therefore not paying for what they needed because the model of delivery wasn't right. But I wouldn't have connected with all those experts and members to be able to step into what was next if I hadn't taken that journey. Failure? I think not. It was the springboard to the success of the next endeavor!

Lessons in the "failures" can be taken in all aspects of life. They are what make us stronger, braver and ready for what's next. Failure is only failure if you walk away, give up and quit.

Dare to learn the lesson.

Lesson 5: Ponder and percolate - or push?

A big lesson is knowing when to ponder and percolate – or push. How do we know when we are on the wrong path or we just need to percolate?

Have you heard the story "three feet from gold", shared by Napoleon Hill in *Think and Grow Rich*? We act, we do the "thing", and we give up because we don't see immediate results. But we are "three feet from gold" and don't know it. We give up just before we hit the sweet spot. If we had kept on doing the thing, we would see the result. But when do we know it's the wrong path versus needing to ponder or percolate?

Unfortunately, I don't have a crystal ball. But I do have magical Millport. When I arrived in June of 2019 for my Scotland sabbatical, I had all my ideas and papers. I'd brought poster paper, notes and folders. I knew there was a book in me to birth. And I sat down to push. I'd made the decision. I was taking decisive bold action, escaping to write – after all, I'd rented a flat in Scotland. But nothing happened. I'd start to write, and my mind would go blank. I struggled. So, I stopped to ponder and percolate.

What I discovered was I was pushing something that wasn't ready. (No surprise to some of you!) I knew what I had in mind, but God had other plans. He wanted me to take a step back and just BE. I needed to ponder and percolate. I needed to get in this magical space – in silence and solitude, stripping away the noise, the chaos and confusion, the expectations and ideas. He had a plan he was working in me. And when I was quiet and ready, the pondering became prolific and the downloads for the book flowed. It took me six out of eight weeks to get to that place before I was ready to write.

If you are pushing, taking decisive bold actions, and nothing is happening, maybe it's time to step back and ponder. Pondering leads to percolation. It may not be the right time. You may need to make a slight adjustment. It may need a little tweak. But you are pushing so hard, you can't see it until you step back.

Faith is not faith until it is acted upon. If you have done the work, the research and the brainstorming, you have the potential to gain tenfold by making the big decisions followed by bold actions. Until you take a step forward and a leap of faith, the doors won't open. But sometimes that leap of faith is to get quiet, ponder and percolate.

Dare to ponder, percolate then push.

Lesson 6: Their approval is not necessary.

As you grow, change and soar, there will be those in your life who simply can't support you. It's not about you – it's about them and their insecurities. There is nothing you can do or say to change them or their opinion. Daring to be you – the real you, means stating your opinion and not playing small just to appease others. That goes from stating what type of food you want for dinner when asked, to the clothes you choose to wear, to business and career decisions, to bigger worldly issues. Not everyone is going to agree with your opinion, your actions or your behaviors. And that's ok. Do you recall Dr. Seuss' famous quote... "Be who you are and say what you feel because those who matter don't mind, and those who mind don't matter."

Here are three important things to remember....

- Don't take it personally. This first agreement of *The 4 Agreements* by Don Miguel Ruiz can be a lifesaver. When the rumors and gossip begin and the person needs to complain, compare and compete, it's them experiencing their issues. It's their own "stuff". While it can be ultra-painful at the time, by releasing those that don't support you, you are opening the door to healthier new relationships.

- Stand up tall, take the high road and don't stoop to their level. While it can be so tempting to fight back or defend yourself, most of the time it's not worth your breath. Yes, there may be circumstances where you need to take it to a higher level, but it's not the norm and please please please, DO NOT wage your war on social media, text or email.

- No approval is necessary. Where did you get the idea that you need their stamp of approval? Why did you decide you needed their permission? You are going to attract a variety of people over your lifetime. But by daring to be you, the real you, you will attract those who are in alignment with your values, ideas and life. Not everyone is going to like you. That's ok, because there are plenty that do!

Here's the bottom line... if you are daring to live your own authentic life, within your values and integrity, who cares what they think? Letting their negative energy pull you down is not what serves you, or them. As hard as it might be to let it go, you must if you want to move forward. Validate and approve of yourself. Don't go looking for it from others. The sooner you can learn to do that, the faster you will find joy in your decisions.

Dare to validate and approve of yourself with no judgement, only love.

Lesson 7: Surrender, accept, pray

Whether you're a person of faith or not, learning to surrender and accept is critical. For me, the prayer is not optional.

We are hit with all kinds of challenges and trials as we move through life. There is nothing meant to be easy about it. There are many lessons to be learned along the way. We hold tight to our "stuff", our failures and flaws, our challenges and setbacks. We hold tight to the stories we've been telling ourselves since we were young. And yet, the only way to freedom is to surrender the "stuff". Let it go. Bless and release it. The people, the business, the marriage, the situation, the money. The tighter we hold it, the more difficult life becomes.

I learned this lesson in many painful ways. I'm sure I still hold on to things too tightly at times, but I hope I've learned to let go a little quicker. My first memorable lesson in this was back in 2013. My son was struggling with drug use and I'd made it my mission to save him. He was a sophomore in high school when we became aware of it and to say I wanted to fix it and control the situation would be an understatement.

How could he do that to me? What would people think? I begged and pleaded with him, I made deals and offers, I screamed, yelled and punished... and I nearly lost myself trying to save him. I began attending AlAnon meetings and put my four agreements into practice even more. Fact was though, until I surrendered, we both suffered. While we'd had him in counseling since becoming aware of his usage, in January of his senior year, we made the very tough decision to have an intervention. No more than an hour later, I got the call that he'd reached out to his counselor for help. Within a few hours, he was picked up for a rehab in Santa Monica.

As I'd shared earlier in this book, I spent the next three days in solitude, crying my eyes out. I felt I'd failed him as a mother. Later, upon reflection, I realized that by truly surrendering, I was able to let go. Surrender, accept and pray. He needed help I couldn't provide. We'd been to hell and back those three years and I truly believe once we surrendered, God intervened by having him ask for help. It became his choice.

Surrender is a daily task. Sometimes hourly. Sometimes moment by moment.

Dare to surrender to God's grace, love and wisdom. Dare to accept the circumstance for what they are, doing what you can, and letting go of the rest. Dare to pray.

Lesson 8: What got you here won't take you there.

What you have been doing for years to get here will not take you where you want to go. Have you heard the definition of insanity? It's doing the same thing over and over again and expecting different results. Sometimes we need to step back and away, quieting our minds and listening with our heart.

When you are considering living your YES and what's next, it's important to get crystal clear. Clarity can be found in the quiet…. silence and solitude. I took a "sabbatical" to Scotland to write this book. I arrived with the flu. Yep – the flu with a fever. Not only that, it was pouring rain, which isn't out of the ordinary for the United Kingdom, but they were putting scaffolding on the building. What? My view!

What I eventually realized was I first had to BE. That scaffolding was a sign of the work the builder needed to do within me. I was blessed to be able to step out of the frenetic pace of Los Angeles, leaving my family, friends and boyfriend behind, to be. I was so caught up in the doing, I was failing to see how I was being called. In week six of eight, this book began to download. But that was only after letting it all go and giving it over. It was a new way of doing things for me. To grow, what I'd been doing was no longer working. I needed to discover what was next.

What is it you need to do to get out of your own way? You may not be able to live abroad, but you can certainly take a day or two for a change of place and pace – and just BE. In the BE-ing, listen for what's next. What is it that needs to change or shift for you to get where you want to go?

Dare to lift it up, give it over and BE. Then, listen. What got you here won't take you there.

CHAPTER 4

....

The YES Method™

How does this all come together? In the YES Method™!

The YES Method™ is the process and formula for daring to live your YES and be you, as fabulous as YOU are! In reviewing the years of my own transformation – the steps, the process, and the tools – I discovered and created The YES Method™. It begins with the YES Wheel and your values. It moves into discovering your yes by digging into the depths of your soul, taking the necessary time to walk the journey, being silent and in solitude to listen and hear that YES calling. Next is to own it – making fear your fuel and taking the lessons from the setbacks. Loving your YES comes when you can fully embrace and commit to it, leaving the excuses behind. Once you have committed, it's designing it – month by month, day by day, goals, steps and tasks. Step 5 in the formula – go out and LIVE it!

Are you ready to begin the work? There is no magic pill or just hoping and wishing things will change in your life. It takes work. The "work" must be done on your own, however I highly recommend asking a trusted friend to join you in this journey, each of you doing your own "work" but sharing as you move along. Not only does this allow for accountability, but also by speaking your dreams and sharing your goals, I believe the Universe will move in ways to support your growth. If you are truly ready to make changes in your life so that you can live your YES, let's begin.

Step 1 - Discover Your YES

Any change or transformation begins in one place... discovery. It may be by accident. It may be a planned strategy. But only in peeling back the layers are we truly able to discover and discern who we are meant to be, what our greater purpose is and how we are to make it happen.

This means sitting in the quiet. It means digging deep and getting really, I mean REALLY honest with yourself. Where is your life now? Are you happy? Are things working? Do you know your path? And the biggest question of all, what are you pretending not to know?

Let's start by reflecting on the various parts of your life.

**Start with the YES Wheel and values exercise,
if you haven't already completed it.**

We've talked about dreaming big and the YES wheel is part of that. Taking stock and getting a "baseline" is the beginning. On the wheel, rate your level of satisfaction in the various areas. Ten means it's perfect (a ten is rare). Zero means it sucks. No one else needs to see your numbers and it's an opportunity to get brutally honest with yourself and your joy levels. If you haven't already downloaded it, it can be found at: www.daretobeyoubook.com

After completing the wheel, the next step is the values exercise. You may have done this many times before, but typically this one takes you a step further – where you put your values into an action sentence. When you are clear on your values, all decisions can be made from a place of aligned strength.

What is on your YES Wheel? In this moment today, what are your areas of highest importance? Why? Ponder or journal your emotional, relational, spiritual, financial and physical pieces in these areas, both personally and professionally.

HOT PEN QUESTIONS: Choose the most important area for today. What is your BIG vision or dream for that one area? What does it look like three years from now? Write it out using as much specificity as you can including the feelings, the relational pieces, the financial impact, where it is and what it looks like. Get as detailed as you can, dreaming BIG! Write it as though it is how you are living in this moment.

Once you have completed this HOT PEN session, re-read it. Does it align with your values? Does it excite you? Have you been brutally honest and transparent with yourself? This is a way to really connect with your inner YES, understanding that dream. Now, speak it – to a confidant, a significant other, your coach or someone else who has earned the right to hear your biggest dreams. If you have partnered with someone during this process, this is the perfect time to share with each other.

Step 2: Own Your YES

Now it's time to own your YES, working through any barriers and obstacles that might be paralyzing you or holding you back. Owning your YES is getting out of your way and moving through the fear, anxiety and doubt. The best way to do this is to make fear your fuel!

What is your greatest fear in living your YES? Fear of failure or success? Fear of comparison, not being good enough or being seen for who you really are? Working through fear, anxiety, ambiguity, comparison and doubt all play into owning your yes. How? One way is by building your confidence in all areas of your life.

Health, finances, business, relationships - where is your brilliance? Where there is confidence there is decisive action and forward movement. It's time to own your fears and navigate through them. But to have confidence, we must peel back the fear. What is the block and why is it so big? Why do you struggle to give yourself permission? Why do you compare?

Become aware of your thoughts and actions – are they feeding your fear? Take the energy you are using to feed the fear and use it as fuel to drive your success. Focus on what's ahead and your big dreams, not what you are leaving behind. Drop the comparison, get past the story you're telling yourself and give yourself permission to achieve and succeed. Let's refocus your energy, time and efforts more positively.

What is your greatest fear? What is holding you back? How would life change for the better by living your YES? What's the worst-case scenario if your fears were realized? What's the best-case scenario if you push past the fear? What are the three biggest obstacles to overcome?

▌▌ **HOT PEN QUESTIONS:** It's time to dig deep. I get it girl-friend - bringing your fears to the surface can be scary. But when they are deeply buried, you can't fight them. Bringing your fears out in the light helps you acknowledge the fear and see they really aren't that scary. As I mentioned before, FEAR is false evidence appearing real. We get in our head, allowing the fear to grab hold of us, and it stops us in our tracks. Until you face it head on, making fear the fuel to fight for your YES, you can get stuck like a deer in the headlights. What is your greatest fear? What is holding you back? How would life change for the better by living your YES? What's the worst-case scenario if your fears were realized? What's the best-case scenario if you push past the fear? What are the three biggest obstacles to overcome?

Step 3: Love Your YES

No time, no money? No excuses!

I've seen and heard them all - the excuses we tell ourselves. But if it's truly a BIG YES for you, then why are you letting the excuses stop you? Yes, it's hard and scary but isn't it worth it? Aren't YOU worth it?

Let's take a closer look. We live in a busy world filled with overwhelm. Maybe your excuse is you truly don't know how to make the time. Here's a place to start. First, review all your activities and determine if they are aligned with your values. Yes, your values. Remember mine are faith, family, freedom and making a difference. Do you remember the story about not going on the field trip with my son (family value) because I was overcommitted? Or was I over obligated?

What's the difference between commitments and obligations? Commitments are things you WANT to do and are committed to. Obligations are everything else. I'm sure you've experienced someone asking you to do something and you get that immediate panic feeling in your gut. You want to say no, you have no interest, you don't have the time, but the person asking is a friend or family member and you feel obligated to say yes. Or maybe FOMO sets in (fear of missing out), so you say yes even though it's not aligned with your core values.

This is where strategic YESes and abundant NOs come in. For every request of your time, attention or money, it's hitting the pause button, reviewing the request in regards to your values and time available, then making a strategic YES answer, or simply saying no. No is a complete sentence. No explanation is needed. There may be opportunities that arise that you'd love to jump into, and you hesitate because of your other commitments. But as you shift to saying yes to the things you are truly committed to and no to the things for which you feel obligated, you'll have more time.

> **HOT PEN QUESTIONS:** When reviewing your current commitments and obligations, are they in alignment with your values? What are your typical excuses? What needs to shift or change? What "obligations" might you release to allow more time for the "commitments" you love? What is the one thing you need to say NO to today to open the time, space or financial resources to say YES?

Step 4: Design Your YES

Now it's time to put pen to paper and commit! You have a big dream in front of you. Big dreams require goals – and goals require tasks. One of the main reasons people don't set goals is that they have not yet accepted responsibility for their life. "Man must cease attributing his problems to his environment and learn again to exercise his will – his personal responsibility." Albert Schweitzer

A few years back I read the book "*Success is Not an Accident*" by Tommy Newberry. I loved his eight rules for setting goals.

1. Highly effective goals are written.

2. Highly effective goals are stated in present tense.

3. Highly effective goals are stated positively.

4. Highly effective goals are consistent with your personal mission statement.

5. Highly effective goals are specific and measurable.

6. Highly effective goals are time bound.

7. Highly effective goals are reasonable and challenging.

8. Highly effective goals are thoroughly planned.

Let's get started with your goals.

HOT PEN QUESTIONS: Start with your big picture. Look three years out. Go back and review the hot pen exercise you completed with the Discover your YES. How can you make that happen? What goals do you need to set for one year out to be able to reach that three-year goal? For example, if I want to buy a house at year three, and I know I need 50k for a down payment, how much do I need to save each month? What do I need to have in the bank at the end of year one? Maybe it's growing a business to a million dollars in three years. That won't happen overnight – so what do you need to have completed by year one to be on your way? More clients? New products? More staff?

Once you know the yearly goals, break the year into 90 day chunks, then one month check-in points, then daily tasks, so that you know every day when you wake up what the one most important thing is that you need to accomplish that day. Maybe it's walking a mile each morning or maybe it's calling three new prospects each day. It's the one thing that MUST get done to move you towards your big dream.

If this seems a bit confusing, visit www.daretobeyoubook.com for more details and instructions.

Step 5: Live Your YES

If you have committed to this process and done the work, results will appear. But results are based on your participation– in YOUR life!

As the CEO of your life, what do you need to be able to move forward into living your YES? Here are the attributes of the CEO:

C:
Courage – to let go of your expectations and be willing to take risks
Consistency – do the one thing daily
Commitment – to the consistency
Community – you can't do it alone

E:

Engagement – in your life and all its opportunities

Energy – participate in self-care to keep your energy up and mind focused

Enthusiasm – face each day with a positive enthusiastic mindset

Encouraging – be gentle, kind and encouraging in your self-talk

O:

Organization – take a moment to simplify and organize your life

Optimization – optimize each task, making it as effective, efficient and useful as possible

Opportunity – be willing and open to the opportunities presented to you

Optimism – start every day with a smile on your face and love in your heart

Living your truth is living your YES – and living your YES is living your truth. It's showing up exactly as you are, who you are meant to be, how you are meant to serve the world and not worrying about what everyone else thinks or expects of you. It's your life – to be lived to the fullest. And while I say all that, it's also not meant to be a selfish, self-centered life. It's serving and supporting as well. But by filling yourself you can fill others, support others, love others – for who they are! Yes, we need to compromise in relationships, yes we need to be aware of other people's feelings, yes we need to be willing to share and discuss. But we also need to be willing to stand our ground, say what we need and not ask permission. The only one responsible for your happiness is YOU. And you are not responsible for someone else's.

We've gone through the full YES Method™ – first the discovery process of peeling back the layers and layers of "stuff", digging deep into the abyss of doubt, fear, shame, guilt, failure, and so much more. But in all of that, hopefully you have owned your yes, facing it head on, working through it rather than burying it deeper. Once you work through it, it's easier to love your yes, replacing those excuses with actionable steps, designing your life with big dreams, bold goals and daily to-dos! All of this leads to living your YES and a better version of you.

PART 2

30 Days of YES

Daring to be you and live your YES is a conscious daily choice. My "your daily yes" posts and emails are meant to support that. We can get off course, forgetting our big why, our big yes, our bold life - if we don't call it to mind daily. Here I've provided 30 days of YES. I've started with a word and maybe a quote, a story, or an idea. It's up to you to take it into your heart. Ponder, journal, meditate or pray – on the meaning for you and how it can help you grow.

After the 30 days is complete, and if you have truly and honestly worked through the Yes Method™ and participated daily, I hope you are starting to see the beginning of your transformation. To continue to support you, I've created the Everything YES website and daily email with inspiration, thoughts and ideas. You can subscribe at www.EverythingYes.Life.

I've chosen to begin the 30 days with Grace, Grit and Gratitude. Why? Because I want to challenge you to live from a place of grace .... forgiveness, humility, kindness, charity; using grit to conquer each day, each challenge; and doing it with gratitude, being grateful for the good as well as the bad, the easy as well as the hard – because only in the challenges do we really learn the lessons.

I look forward to hearing from you as you create your rituals and routines around daring to be you and living your YES.

Day 1

GRACE

"Unexpected kindness is the most powerful, least costly and most underrated agent of human change."
—BOB KERREY

Grace can be defined as extending kindness to the unworthy. Synonyms include kindness, kindliness and love. My belief in a loving God allows me to feel and experience grace and mercy, which in turn, gives me the opportunity to grow from my mistakes. My faith allows me to believe in grace and blessings despite the fact I don't deserve them.

You are given grace as well. You may not be aware of it or feel it, but grace is there for the asking. And you can offer that grace to others... extending forgiveness, kindness and humility.

Dare to give and receive grace.

Can you extend grace to someone who may need it today? Maybe even yourself? You have the power to make someone's day, even your own.

Day 2

GRIT

"Do one thing every day that scares you."
—Eleanor Roosevelt

Grit is defined by strength and firmness of character; indomitable spirit; courage and resolve. Grit is when the going gets tough, the tough get it done. It's the epitome of living with the mantra YES I CAN.

We all face daily challenges – big and small. We may want to curl up and push the world out. And that may be ok – for a minute or two. But those who stand back up, dust themselves off, put their big girl panties on and take the next step will get through to the other side. Grit requires courage, tenacity, fortitude and moxie!

Dare to find your own mantra – or use YES I CAN – when the challenges arise.

How do you use "grit" in your daily life? What is your mantra for when the going gets tough?

Day 3

GRATITUDE

A YES woman lives in gratitude. She is blessed with peaks and valleys,
trials and triumphs, challenges and celebrations –
and is grateful for the lessons in all of them.

Gratitude comes easy on the good days – and can be almost impossible to be found on the bad. I truly believe there is a lesson to be learned in every setback, challenge and failure. Some lessons I'd rather have not experienced in the way I did. Some days my gratitude was only that the sun was shining – that was all I could be grateful for in that moment. But living in a place of unconditional gratitude allowed me to get out of my own way and grow.

Life may be throwing you a curve ball or challenges you never saw coming. It might be an illness, a failed relationship, the death of a loved one or a struggling career. But if you can find gratitude for the littlest thing, even the fact that the sun rose again today, you just may find a new perspective in how you see your challenges.

Dare to be grateful for all things.

What are three things you are most grateful for today? Continue to practice the "three gratitudes" each day.

Day 4

GOD OR FAITH

*A YES woman has faith – that while she cannot see the next step,
she's willing and trusts herself to make the move.*

Do you believe in a power greater than yourself? Do you know God? I do. But no matter your beliefs, please don't let that stop you from reading. He – or She – has many "names" including God or Source or the Universe, Buddha, the Divine and many others. I believe in a higher power and for me that Higher Power is God. He has shown his grace and mercy to me more than once. He has given me signs and messages in the form of friends and circumstances. I've seen it written in the sky and written on a chain link fence. I've had dreams and downloads and when I am quiet, I can sometimes hear that still small voice that is God. It means life is not always sunshine and roses, but no matter what, I am not alone.

Growing up, my family attended church every Sunday. My grandfather was a Presbyterian minister and church was a "requirement' each week. However, it wasn't until later in life that I truly understood the opportunity to have a relationship with God. Yes, a relationship. Knowing God is much more then attending church on Sunday. It's being aware of the signs and allowing him to walk by your side every single day.

One of my most memorable messages was quite literally on a chain link fence. It was a particularly difficult day – we were hosting a big family function, but it became a day in which my marriage was clearly coming to an end. Upon leaving my daughters at the event and driving to the airport, I struggled to hold back the tears. We began the turn onto the freeway and attached to a chain link fence at the on-ramp was a banner... "God Loves You." I was immediately filled with peace. I knew he was there, and I would be ok. When I shared that experience, I was asked "and you think that was for you?" I undoubtedly knew it was - a sign, a message of love in one of my most difficult moments. I was not alone. Whatever your beliefs, know that you are loved and not alone.

Dare to have faith.

Do you believe in something greater than yourself? If so, how do you connect with your Higher Power daily?

Day 5

FEAR

"Everything you've ever wanted is on the other side of fear."
—GEORGE ADDAIR

A YES woman faces her fears, getting comfortable being uncomfortable.

Fear can take us from a place of grace and gratitude to chaos and panic, in an instant. It can also put us into a place of negative reactivity rather than positive response. Have you heard the saying or acronym; FEAR – False Evidence Appearing Real. Things seem one way as being real but when you take a step back you understand there is nothing to fear at all.

How many times have you made a decision based in fear, that then turned out to be the wrong decision? Shortly after separating from my x-husband, I went into full blown fear of financial loss. I'd been an entrepreneur for 20+ years and yet my fear of supporting myself drove me to take a part-time job paying minimum wage. Did I really think a minimum wage job was going to meet my financial needs? And even funnier, after being an entrepreneur for over 20+ years, could I really work for someone else? I quit the job after three weeks, grateful to my employer and the lesson I'd learned. I then took it upon myself to become empowered with knowledge to take control of my financial foundation.

Be aware of fear and its grip, then do what you can to remember to be grateful even in the scariest moments. Let go of fear and make it your fuel... fuel to become empowered in the knowledge of what you are fearing and the tools to face it head on.

Dare to face your greatest fears.

What is your greatest fear? Financial? Relational? Health? When faced with this fear, how have you reacted in negativity? Now that you know fear can be made into your fuel, what is one thing you can do to empower yourself to face this fear head on?

Day 6

DENIAL

What are you pretending not to know?

That question has been a sobering one for me, more than once in my life. But the first time I was asked that question, I was sitting in a hotel room with a group of women who knew me well. What was the answer? That my marriage was over. (mic drop.) I had been in denial for years. I hadn't faced the facts and it was easier to pretend not to know.

Denial is a shock-absorber for the soul. It gives you a moment to come to grips with what you are facing. But until denial moves to awareness and eventually acceptance, you will be stuck. Awareness is painful. Acceptance requires grace.

Dare to ask yourself the question... and find the answer.

What are you pretending not to know?...

Day 7

WORRY

"Worry is a waste of energy. It can't change the past. It can't control the future. It only makes today miserable."
— RICK WARREN

We all worry... but it truly serves nothing and no one. I love the quote above from Rick Warren. It says it all. Worrying about something that happened in the past is a waste. Nothing can be done to change it. Worrying to control the future is like thinking you have superpowers. While we can do our best to make the decision in the moment for the future, we can't control the outcome. Worrying make things miserable now.

I've been on the worry-train before – wrapped up in trying to create a different outcome. It drained me of all energy, made me physically sick, and for what? When I feel the worry begin to rise within, I do my best to make that conscious choice to let go, let God - and become grounded in grace and gratitude for what the opportunity could be!

Dare to let go of worry and get grounded in grace and gratitude

What are you most worried about? How is the worry serving you? What could you do to let go and trust?

Day 8

HUMILITY

"Humility is not thinking less of yourself, it's thinking of yourself less."
—RICK WARREN

I've been knocked down in the ring too many times to count, but never knocked out. I am a fighter who does her best to stand back up with grace, humility and gratitude. But that wasn't always the case.

While raising our children, we lived in an affluent community. Problem was, everyone would compare, judge and compete. I was no different. I shudder to think at the judgement I levied on others. And my sincere apologies to anyone affected by my poor behavior.

When my son began to struggle, we quickly became the focus of much judgement. In fact, we had a woman from the Department of Children and Family Services knock on our door one afternoon. Someone had reported us for investigation. She sat my teenagers down at the dining room table for questions then toured our house. I can't begin to share how horrible and humiliating it was.

While I know karma goes around and comes around, I was reminded in such a painful way not to judge others or compare my circumstances. I had to dig very deep to find humility in humiliation and I have taken that lesson forward.

Dare to be humble.

How can you dare to be humble? Have you judged others? Most of us have at one time or another. How can you show humility and kindness, today and every day?

Day 9

FORGIVENESS

*Holding a grudge or resentment is like drinking the poison
and expecting the other person to die.*

Everyone experiences hurt, betrayal or something they think they can never forgive. I know I have and certainly more than once. As the quote above suggests, when we hold on to the hurt, grudge or resentment, we become the victim, not only in our heart but more importantly, in our body. We stress about it, ruminate on it, contemplate how we can return the hurt. We get angry, depressed and a whole list of other things. Bottom line, holding on to the hurt, hurts us.

Years ago, I experienced a betrayal from someone I thought was a friend. It involved not only me, but my children and family. I stressed, I cried, I screamed, and I thought about all the ways I could hurt her as she had hurt me. All the hate and anger took me to a very dark place. As I worked through the betrayal and learned more about me and my YES, including attending AlAnon meetings, I soon realized I needed to forgive her. I didn't need to forget it, and I wasn't going to have a conversation with her, but I needed to bless and release it. I went into a special favorite church, lit a candle, albeit a battery operated one, and sat down to pray. The tears flowed and the heavy weight lifted. As I stood up to leave, I glanced at the candle. It was no longer lighted. In that moment, that God wink moment, I knew all was forgiven, blessed and released.

Note: Please know, I understand there are things that can never be forgotten. But blessing and releasing the hurt and forgiving the other person allows you to move on.

Dare to forgive.

Who do you need to forgive? Do you need forgiveness? Bless and release the anger, guilt and frustration. One way is to write a letter to the person, pouring all your feelings out on paper – then DO NOT send it but rather burn or shred it. Or maybe it is time to reach out to them for a conversation? Look into your heart. You know what you need to do.

Day 10

RESISTANCE

"Sometimes the bad things that happen in our lives put us directly on the path to the best things that will ever happen to us."
—Nicole Reed

What are you resisting? Why are you resisting? Sometimes we resist out of fear. Sometimes it's the unknown. But the more we resist, the more it persists.

Are you resistant to change? You know you want something different; you want a change in a relationship or career, but you become resistant. I work with many entrepreneurs who want to make a change – in their business or personal life. But they become resistant to hear the ideas, suggestions and work it will take. Change is scary. The work it requires can be harder to grasp and accept then the hope of something better. But growth doesn't happen without letting go of the resistance and stepping into the new ideas.

Dare to release resistance.

What are you resisting? Why? How would life change for the better if you were to lean into the change, releasing the resistance and allowing the flow?

Day 11

CHILDREN AND THE INNER CHILD

A YES woman honors her inner child. She colors outside the lines, thinks outside the box and lives outside the limits of her fears.

Children. A most precious gift. I am so grateful for them. They bless my life in so many ways, including being reminded to play and have fun! Whether you have birthed a child, adopted a child, are an aunt or uncle or have a fur baby, strive to find your inner child. Childlike behavior allows the playful fun to come out.

Have you ever ridden a scooter? While staying in Millport Scotland, I had a child-like urge to rent a scooter and ride all the way around the island. Months previously I had ridden a bike around the 10.2-mile road and that was "work", but certainly worth it for the beautiful views and sense of accomplishment. But this particular day, it was a bit cooler, the wind was blowing, and I had this intuitive moment to just go do it.

As I stood in front of the line-up of scooters for rent, I began playing the tape in my head. What if I fall? What if I get hurt? I've never ridden a scooter – would I be able to keep my balance. Well let me tell you, it was the most incredible hour and a half. The wind in my hair, the sun on my face, the green hills all around, the white caps on the ocean… I felt wild and free. I was giddy with laughter as I scootered along. I even stopped at the only café on the backside of the island and treated myself to tea and cake. It was a day I will not soon forget and will most definitely repeat.

Dare to find your inner child and play!

How can you put childlike fun into your life? Is there something you have put off doing? Stop by a park and get on the swing, take an art class and paint with your fingers, sign up for those dance classes. Whatever it is, do something that makes you giddy with laughter and filled with joy.

Day 12

VALIDATION

"I am who I am. Your approval is not necessary."

You are perfect just as you are. Be grateful for your quirks and imperfections. Have grace when being critical of your flaws. Understand that looking for approval from others serves no one and often leads to disappointment. Self-validation is all you truly need.

This was a long-fought lesson – and at times it still roars its ugly head. Why did I have such a need for validation from others – on my choices, my decisions, my looks, my life. Over the years, I looked for others to validate I was successful, I was pretty, I was smart, I was worthy. And as you can imagine, the expectations were almost always dashed. I had to learn the skill of validating myself – my decisions, my choices, my success.

I don't need anyone to give me permission to be me. I don't need anyone to approve of my choices or decisions. I will answer to my Higher Power while doing what I feel called to do. I will not play small because someone else says I should. I will live my purpose. I am me.

Dare to validate yourself – your choices, your decisions, your image, your success.

Who are you searching for to validate you? Is it a constant need to be validated? What if you look to yourself, your inner knowing? You don't need anyone to give you permission to be you.

Day 13

SELF-LOVE

"Love yourself first, and everything falls into line."
—LUCILLE BALL

Is there a dark space or an empty hole that you are trying to fill? You look into the abyss, can't see the bottom and you start pouring into it. Why do we feel we must fill the hole? Why do we try to fill it with food, alcohol, drugs, sex, shopping, social media, unhealthy relationships and more? Is it uncomfortable? Of course. But the ONLY way to truly fill it and feel whole is unconditional self-love.

Instead of looking for love from a special "someone", give love freely and unconditionally to yourself with no judgement and no expectations… just gentle kindness. Unconditional self-love is the hardest thing to give. We have expectations, judgement, shame… and don't feel worthy.

I spent many years looking for someone to "love" me the way I wanted to be loved. Truth is, until I began working on fiercely loving myself, accepting myself, releasing the judgement and giving myself a hug, I couldn't give unconditional love to others. Once you fill that hole with unconditional self-love, you can pour that unconditional love into others.

Dare to love yourself unconditionally!!

How do you practice self-love? What can you do today to express that love to yourself? And then share it with others.

Day 14

PRESENCE

*"Yesterday's the past, tomorrow's the future, but today is a gift.
That's why it's called the present."*
—BIL KEANE

Are you present? I mean REALLY present and aware of all that surrounds you, right here, right now? The beauty in a sunset, the glorious wildflowers in bloom, a quick hug or kiss or smile, a short text, a heartfelt thank you.... Are you present enough to notice, and then express gratitude for the little things?

In this world of crazy fast-paced chaos, it's easy to lose ourselves in being busy and doing and forget to just BE. As an example, let's talk about how connected we have become to our phones. They seem to go with us everywhere. They are at the dinner table, the bedside table and heck, if we are honest, the bathroom. What if for a moment or two, we put the phone down. I promise you, the world will not come to an end, that client doesn't need your immediate response, and your 5000 "friends" can hold their breath while they wait for your next post.

But seriously, I've made a choice and effort to put my phone down and get present. If I'm with my boyfriend, my girlfriends, my kids, my parents, my clients.... I want to be present with them. Set your boundaries. And if you are together with someone else who can't seem to put their phone down, maybe ask them why and what's so important that they can't be present with you.

Dare to get present in your life,
in this moment. It's a gift.

When you truly get present to the here and now, not yesterday or tomorrow, you can experience joy in a much deeper way. What can you do today to become more present?

Day 15

B-WHO-U-R

"I love who I've become because I fought for her."

A YES woman stands in her power, owns her brilliance and never needs to wear a mask.

Do you show up as you really are? Or are you trying to be something or someone you aren't? It took me almost 50 years to become me. Daring to be you and living your YES is living your truth. If you aren't willing to be exactly who you are, without the façade or people pleasing, you can't be the real you.

I love bling. Sparkly, shiny bling. Several years ago, I bought the most amazing pair of black cowgirl boots with black shiny sequins. I don't live in Texas, but I do love country music and bling. The first time I put on my new boots to wear them in Los Angeles, I was asked "Are you really going to wear those out in public?" I might as well have been punched in the gut. I took my boots off, put on other shoes, and walked out the door. I allowed someone else to dictate who I was that night.

Dare to be YOU!

Are you living and speaking your YES, your truth? Are you being exactly who you are or are you pretending to be someone different in the hopes of fitting in, being liked or loved or accepted? What can you do today to stand up and be proud of WHO-U-R?

Day 16

PEACE

"Do not let the behavior of others destroy your inner peace."
—DALAI LAMA

Peace. Where is it and how do we keep it, especially in this world that seems to breed chaos, anxiety and ambiguity? Yes, peace can be found in silence and solitude, but also deep within our soul once we accept our circumstances.

Have you ever had a moment where you felt totally out of control of your circumstances? (Silly question I know.) The chaos of life is banging on every proverbial door and you feel you just need to shut the world out for a minute. Then you are stopped in your tracks... becoming aware of where you are, who is around or maybe something beautiful. You take a deep breath and feel a calm wash over you. That is peace.

I've experienced God's peace more than once in my life – and over the last few years I've learned to allow the peace more and more. Learning to BE instead of DO is the place to start. Being quiet and alone can help. Listening and allowing, feeling and awareness. Your intuition will show you the peace that surrounds you.

Dare to find peace in the chaos.

How are you letting the outside world dictate your inner peace? What can you do to be aware and bring yourself back to center? What brings you a feeling of peace, calm and tranquility? How can you find it through-out your day?

Day 17

OPPORTUNITY

The pessimist sees difficulty in every opportunity.
The optimist sees the opportunity in every difficulty.
—WINSTON CHURCHILL

When one door closes, another one opens.

Opportunity knocks. Do you answer? Fear can stop us. Doubt can too. But when the stars align and prayers are answered, do you say YES?

Over the years, I've had many opportunities knock on my door. Some have been business related such as traveling and speaking in different parts of the country with no real understanding of what the outcome will be. Other times I've been presented opportunities that seemed Divinely inspired. But is there a reason it's given?

One such opportunity was purchasing the flat in Scotland. The flat I lived in and loved for three months – I was offered the opportunity to buy it. And not just the usual opportunity but one that was in a pay-it-forward kind of way. Was it scary to say yes? Absolutely! Did some see it as crazy? You bet! Did I know in my heart it was the right opportunity for me? YES, I did. Do I now own a flat in Scotland? YES, I do!

Dare to say YES to an unexpected opportunity.

What opportunity is at your door? Why are you saying no? Is it fear and doubt, even though the stars aligned for the opportunity to even be available? Take a second look and maybe open the new door.

Day 18

HOME

"Home is where love resides, memories are created, friends always belong, and laughter never ends."
—ANONYMOUS

Home. Sure, there is the nostalgic place where we grew up, with good and sometimes not so good memories. As we've grown, there may be new homes filled with laughter, love and friends. But truly, home is wherever your heart is. It's not the stuff that makes it. It's not the location. It's the love with which it is filled.

I've lived in over nine places in my lifetime – only a few of which truly felt like home. The home we raised our children in has the most memories for me. When we divorced, we sold the home. I was crushed. It was my forever home, or so I thought. But what I quickly realized was I could create home wherever I am. It's with pictures, people, parties, laughter and love. I love where I live because I've made it my home. And you can too.

Dare to create a home wherever you live.

Is your heart in your home? Have you created a space you love to spend time, that renews and reenergizes you? Do you invite others into your home? How can you create a home you love – or add to the one you have now?

Day 19

SUPPORT

If you want to go fast, go alone. If you want to go far, go together.
—African Proverb

Support. It goes without saying that support is critical in all areas of our life. Family, friends, business associates, significant others, children. Sometimes it is given freely, other times WE MUST ASK.

I am grateful for all the support I've received over the years. And I've learned that it's ok to ask as well. There is no weakness in it - in fact, it takes great strength and courage to ask for support. Don't go it alone. ASK.

Dare to ask for support.

What areas of your life are you trying to go it alone and faltering? When you look at your goals and dreams, where could you use the most support? Who could you ask for it? Reach out... chances are high they will say yes.

Day 20

SIMPLIFY

"Voluntary simplicity means going fewer places in one day rather than more, seeing less so I can see more, doing less so I can do more, acquiring less so I can have more."
— Jon Kabat Zinn

"Aspire not to have more but to be more." – Oscar Romero

We live in a fast-paced world filled with things to make life quick and easy. We also fall prey to the desire of more stuff, more time, more people, more everything. But sometimes all those short-cuts and "mores" get in the way of living a simple life. We shop in warehouse stores buying months' worth of toilet paper, order coffee to go rarely taking a moment to sit and enjoy it and have to-do lists that are multiple pages long.

My summer in Scotland reminded me of the value and benefit of simplifying life. I came for two months and stayed for three. I had one large suitcase and one small. The weather is unpredictable and a warm coat as well as raincoats are a must. But in reality, I wore a handful of the clothing I brought. I walked to the store for a day or two worth of food. My kitchen had two pans, a pot, dishes for four and wine glasses. What am I getting at here? All the other "stuff" back home that I didn't miss one bit.

I'm in a season of purging, simplifying and preparing. Purging the old, simplifying the present and preparing for the future. Happiness comes when our hearts are filled with joy and contentment in who we are and what we have, not in needing all the extra fluff and "stuff".

Dare to simplify your life.

How can you simplify your life? Is it less "stuff" or getting out of the fast-paced quick and easy? Can you start by cleaning out a drawer or closet? How about the garage? Can you say no to some of the multiple things on your to-do lists? Can you take a moment to sit and sip your hot beverage... being in the moment?

Day 21

SERVICE

*"The best way to find yourself is to lose yourself
in the service of others."*
—MAHATMA GANDHI

Serving others provides you grace, humility, gratitude and joy. There is nothing better than helping someone else and being of service. And being of service doesn't require a grand commitment. It's found in even the littlest actions.

This can be as easy as smiling and saying hello as you pass someone on the street or as complex as volunteering to chair a non-profit philanthropy event. I've done both! I have a friend who makes a point of saying "Hell-OOO" in her beautiful Scottish accent to everyone she passes. Even when someone is looking down or away, she will greet them in her cheery sweet voice. Do you think it might make someone's day? You bet! Could you? YES.

Dare to be of service.

How can you be of service? Is it the daily small things like a smile and hello? How about the bigger service opportunities like volunteering for your favorite cause or charity? Find something you're passionate about and become of service.

Day 22

RITUALS AND ROUTINES

*"You will never change your life until you change something you do
daily. The secret of your success is found in your daily routine."*
—John C. Maxwell

Routines and Rituals. What are yours? I begin every morning with reading, praying and journaling. Like brushing my teeth, this is essential to
me. When something comes up and I'm unable to practice my routine,
I feel it. I am wobbly, uncentered and ungrounded. But when I do practice my routine daily, peace and tranquility abound throughout my day.

Dare to create rituals and routines.

What can you do to create a ritual and routine? From reading or
journaling to …what is it for you? It's a daily habit that serves in keeping you grounded to your greater purpose.

Day 23

RELATIONSHIPS

"The best and most beautiful things in this world cannot be seen or even heard but must be felt with the heart."
—HELEN KELLER

Whether a love relationship or friendship, with a man or woman, we need to nurture our relationships. We cannot survive without human connection. It's time to look at the relationships that are most important and make sure you are doing your part.

A few years ago, I discovered the book *"The 5 Love Languages"* by Gary Chapman. There is a quiz to help you discover your love language and for those close to you to discover theirs. One of my daughter's top love languages is gifts. Missing her birthday would be a crime. But it's not in getting her some extravagant gift, it's in receiving even just a card. She feels my love when I do something special, like send a card out of the blue, make cookies and mail them to her, remember her birthday and send something special or even just send a love text message.

My love language is physical touch and quality time. Time spent together means the most to me, doing something fun or just hanging out. When you know your love language and can share it with those you love, and vice versa, everyone gets filled with love in a way they can understand.

Dare to nurture your relationships.

What can you do today to nurture a relationship? A quick phone call, a text message, or maybe sending a card in the mail! Maybe it's preparing a special meal or sharing a kiss. Take a moment to reach out to someone you care about!

Interested in learning your love language? You can find the quiz at: www.5lovelanguages.com.

Day 24

JOY

"The tragedy of life is not that it ends so soon,
but that we wait so long to begin it."
—W.M. LEWIS

Life. It's short. It's precious. Every day is a gift. I have a few friends who have recently lost parents. We hope for more time, we grasp on to the memories, and we pray for peace. Let this be a reminder to be present, in every moment of life, being in gratitude and finding joy in the time we have together here on earth.

What about your life? There is a wonderful quote from the movie *The Bucket List*. Near the end of the movie, Morgan Freeman tells Jack Nicholson there are two questions to ask yourself at the end of your life... 1. Have you found joy in your life? 2. Has your life brought joy to others? Powerful. I don't know about you, but I want to be able to answer a resounding YES to those two questions. I don't want to be at the end of my life saying I "woulda, coulda, shoulda". Joy can be found in so many things if you are looking. And bringing joy to others should be a daily to-do.

Dare to LIVE life to the fullest!

Have you found joy in your life? If not, why not? Do you bring joy to others, daily? If not, how can you do that starting today?

Day 25

PATIENCE

*"The hardest test in life is to have the patience to wait
for the right moment."*
—Anonymous

Patience. Do you have any? In a world of instant gratification, it can be a challenge. No one wants to sit and sift through the "stuff". We don't want to slow down or let it pass. Without patience, we try to control things that are simply not up to us. Then we get into fear and anxiety because we have no control, which then leads to lack of patience and sometimes anger.

Travel is a good place to bring a lot patience. Whether business or pleasure, I've always seen travel as a gift. With the amount of security, slow downs and delays, without patience, travel can become a nightmare. On a recent trip between the states and Europe, there was a couple wearing matching t-shirts that read, instead of the usual *keep calm and carry on*, "I won't keep calm and you can F*@K off." Wow! So much for patience! But it just reminded me of the lack of patience our society breeds. Patience for each other, patience for success and patience to wait for the right moment.

Things don't always work out the way we want. Or maybe things aren't working as fast in your life as you'd like. But if we allow grace to fuel our patience.... gratitude will follow.

Dare to be patient.

Is there an area in your life where patience is lacking? Do you have expectations that are simply unreasonable? What would happen if you were to allow grace to fuel your patience?

Day 26

BLESS AND RELEASE

"Some people believe holding on and hanging in there are signs of great strength. However, there are times when it takes much more strength to know when to let go and then do it."
—ANN LANDERS

Bless and Release. It's a skill. It's a challenge. It takes monumental strength. But it's something that will clear the mind and soul. We hold on to things past their "due" date, we have expectations that may never be met - but if we can learn to accept and be grateful for the lesson and leave the rest, how much lighter and happier we will be. Bless the person, the problem, the situation - and with grace, release it. Do not be weighed down by the burden. It is not yours to carry.

Dare to bless and release.

What is it that you need to bless and release? What are you holding on to past its "due" date? How would the weight be lifted, and your life transformed if you were able to let it go?

BALANCE

"Never get so busy making a living that you forget to make a life."
—DOLLY PARTON

Balance can be elusive. And in fact, by society's definition, impossible. But I'd like to challenge you to look at balance as integration. We look at work/life balance and think everything in equal parts. But truly, balance or integration is bringing together your desires based on your values, commitments and interests along with your time.

When I had my magazine business, I knew I had seasons of a crazy busy work life. Deadlines were hard and fast, and it was up to me to find the balance between my work life and home life. But I knew while early spring was always the craziest time for my event business, things would lighten up and summer was my time to play with my kids. It wasn't a daily balance. It was an ebb and flow throughout the year. As an entrepreneur, there is start up time, launch time, growth time, crazy time and down time. I've been there and done that, more than once. Integrating work life within your daily life is a choice. Find balance that works for you – not how it's defined by your friend, your neighbor or society at large.

Dare to re-define balance and find integration.

Are you so busy working that you are missing out on your life? Do you compare yourself to the family next door or the mom you work with? Finding balance or integration is an inside job. It starts by looking at your values, then what you are committed to and those priorities, and making tough decisions and hard choices. But it's your decisions and choices.

HAPPINESS

"Happiness is not something ready-made.
It comes from your own actions."
—DALAI LAMA

A YES woman finds happiness. She does not leave it to chance or expect someone else to give it to her.

Finding true happiness begins with finding yourself. Who are you, what do you want, what are your values in life? No one else can do it for you - it's an inside job. Fall in love with you. Happiness will appear when you trust and release your expectations.

Dare to create your happiness.

How do you define happiness? Are you happy? What's one thing you can do today to create more happiness in your daily life?

Day 29

FREEDOM

"Be who you want to be, not what others want to see.
Be true. Be unique. Be free."
—ANONYMOUS

How do you define freedom? It's one of my core values. Freedom in my work life, my family life and my play life. Freedom to make decisions based on my values, my interests, and my commitments. Freedom to work from Los Angeles or work from Scotland. Freedom to be me.

It took me almost 50 years to understand the importance of freedom in my life. While I always had freedom in parts of my life, I was also one who worked to appease everyone else, sacrificing my freedom in decisions, finances, relationships and more. As I've gotten older, freedom in being able to make decisions from my heart (not always my head) has been free-ing and empowering. I'm not suggesting reckless abandon – but I am suggesting finding that freedom for you.

Dare to be true, be unique, and be free.

Are you free to be the real you? Do you have the freedom you desire? How can you practice freedom in your life?

Day 30

COURAGE AND BRAVERY

"It takes courage to grow up and become who you really are."
—E.E. Cummings

Being courageous and brave enables one to face difficult situations and work through them. In the last few years I've signed divorce papers, bought my own car, sold a house, moved into a new home, traveled the globe, started over financially and began a new chapter of my life. To say it's been a roller coaster of emotions would be an understatement. But being courageous and committed to living it from a place of grace and gratitude every single day is what not only gets me through but has allowed me to find true happiness.

As E.E. Cummings' quote above states it takes great courage to grow up and become who you really are. Living your YES = living your truth = being exactly who you are. It takes great courage to be YOU!

Dare to be courageous and brave!

Are you being brave? Have you gathered up the courage to be YOU – in all your glory, exactly as you are meant to be? Stand up tall girlfriend – you were born to be brave, bold and fabulous!

Resources

Throughout this book, I refer to a variety of other books, services and more. Here you will find website links, book titles and recommended reading. While technology and the web are ever-changing, these urls were working as of this book's publication.

Al-Anon – www.al-anon.org

Daring Greatly by Brene Brown

The Four Agreements by don Miguel Ruiz

The 5 Love Languages by Gary Chapman
www.5lovelanguages.com

The Gifts of Imperfection by Brene Brown

Success is Not an Accident by Tommy Newberry

Work with Cathy: Are you ready to take a deeper dive and need a coach to assist? Cathy has many products, programs and events to help support you in living your YES. Details can be found on her website – www.CathyAlessandra.com

About the Author

Cathy Alessandra, also known as The YES I CAN Coach, is a dynamic, innovative woman who inspires her clients and audiences into action. An entrepreneur for over 23 + years, Cathy has owned and published two magazines and has two best-selling books on Amazon with this being her third. She coaches entrepreneurs around the world using her signature YES Method™ and Success System. Cathy's energetic style provides an interactive experience for business owners who want to take their business and life to the next level. She shares her expertise on topics ranging from marketing and networking to leadership and work-life balance.

Acclaimed as a "marketing guru" by her clients, Cathy is the CEO of Alessandra Group LLC and has been featured on CBS.com, career-intelligence.com and KFWB news radio in Los Angeles among others. She was nominated for the Los Angeles Business Journal 2015 "Women Making a Difference" award and others as well as receiving the President's Call to Service Life-Time Achievement award for her philanthropic work. She is a Certified Business and Life Coach with the International Coach Federation but more importantly, she has "been there", "done that" and "walks her talk". Her stories of challenge to celebration and struggle to success along with her implementable tips, tools and tricks will inspire all who know her to say YES I CAN to creating a business and life they love.

Cathy lives bi-continentally, spending time in her homes in Los Angeles and Scotland. She has three grown children and a grand-dog named Rosie.

A few final thoughts...

Living your YES is a daily undertaking. It's not easy, but it's not hard either. It takes you, showing up as best you can every day, living, loving and speaking your truth, daring to be the real you.

Here are a few key points to remember:

- Know what you want and allow yourself to have it. Set the intention.

- Step into your life. Commit, then figure it out.

- Intensely focus on the essentials. What's the one thing you need to do TODAY.

- Don't be attached to the outcome. This or better.

- Invest in yourself. Whether a life or business coach, a therapist, or a support group, invest in you.

- Find your tribe. I cannot stress this enough. You cannot, nor should you, do life alone.

- Keep moving. There is no failure, only lessons (unless you quit).

- Be magnetic. Have confidence, enthusiasm and face every day with a smile.

- Trust and have faith.

Dare to be YOU – in everything you do. After all, you were born to be brave, bold and fabulous!

Celtic Blessing

May the road rise up to meet you.
May the wind always be at your back.
May the sun shine warm upon your face,
and rains fall soft upon your fields,
and until we meet again,
may God hold you in the palm of his hand.

Made in the USA
San Bernardino, CA
13 November 2019